W9-CBM-079

YES SHE DID!

MEDICINE

Yes She Did! Medicine

Copyright © 2015
Published by Lightswitch Learning
Written by Jordan McCreary

Printed in Dominican Republic.

Lightswitch Learning
250 East 54th Street, Suite P2
New York, NY 10022

Educators and Librarians, for a variety of teaching resources,
visit www.lightswitchlearning.com

ISBN: 978-1-61570-932-8

TABLE OF CONTENTS

CHAPTER 1
INTRODUCTION

Picture yourself standing in line at Disney World on a hot day, about to get on your favorite roller coaster.

Everybody around you is excited, eager to get out of the heat and onto the ride. Suddenly, the girl in front of you falls to the ground unconscious. Nobody knows what to do.

SAVING THE DAY

Not long ago, women were not allowed to work in medicine. Today, these women are saving lives daily as paramedics.

Someone calls an ambulance, and the paramedics arrive.

Telling everyone to step back, they perform CPR on the girl, bringing her back into consciousness. Then they pick her up off the ground, lift her into the ambulance, and rush her to the hospital. This is the kind of situation that Tracey Loscar faces every day. Tracey is a paramedic for the University Hospital Emergency Medical Services. It is her job to ride in an ambulance and help people in medical emergencies. However, women like Tracey were not always allowed to be paramedics. In fact, if it wasn't for the work of a young schoolteacher named Elizabeth Blackwell, women would never have had the opportunities in medicine that they have today.

"Medicine" is a term that can be described as the art and science of healing. The field of modern medicine is made up of doctors, nurses, and other health professionals like dentists and pharmacists. Throughout history, most people who worked in medicine were men. Women weren't allowed to receive medical education and could only be caregivers. This means that they couldn't actually treat people when they were sick—only comfort them. When the first woman in America graduated from medical school in 1849, the road to gender equality in medicine began.

Elizabeth Blackwell was born in England in 1821. Her father was very strict about education. He believed that each of his children should have the opportunity to develop their unique talents. Growing up, Elizabeth had a governess (a private schoolteacher) and multiple tutors to help her succeed. When she moved to America with her family at age 11, her father became involved in the anti-slavery movement. This was her first experience with civil rights, which would eventually help lead her to fight for women's rights. Elizabeth's father instilled many important values in her, like hard work, courage, and independence. When he died suddenly in 1838, she had to draw upon those skills and become an independent woman.

As the first female doctor in America, it may seem weird that Elizabeth was originally disgusted by medicine. In her book *Pioneering Work in Opening the Medical Profession to Women,* she said that she "hated everything connected with the body, and could not bear the sight of a medical book." Her opinion changed when her friend began dying from a painful disease. This friend told her that she would have been much more comfortable if her doctor had been a wom-

STAMPED FOR SUCCESS

Elizabeth quickly became one of the most famous women in America. She was even featured on a U.S. postage stamp.

an. This, along with her desire to live an independent life, caused Elizabeth to choose medicine. Now, she just needed to get into medical school.

When Elizabeth was applying to medical schools,

THE FEMALE PHYSICIAN

Thanks to Elizabeth's pioneering work, women are finally achieving equality in medicine.

many doctors told her that she couldn't do it. They told her to go to Europe to study, and even to disguise herself as a man. She faced many rejections, but was eventually accepted into Geneva Medical College in 1847. This was not an easy feat, however. The faculty at the school were not sure if they should accept her because she was a woman. So they put Elizabeth's acceptance up to a vote. Her future was in the hands of the staff—150 men. If just one of them said "no," she would be turned away. The men thought it was a joke, so they all voted to accept her. Imagine their surprise when she showed up for class! Two years later, thanks to a vote that might never have been, Elizabeth Blackwell became the first American medical doctor. Her hard work, dedication, and perseverance paved the way for women everywhere to pursue their dreams in medicine.

DID YOU KNOW...

Elizabeth was rejected by 16 medical schools before she was accepted into Geneva Medical College. After her success as a doctor, she opened a medical college for women so they wouldn't have to face the same hardship she did.

CHAPTER 2
PHYSICIANS

Physicians, or "doctors," are the most common medical workers that we come across. Physicians have many jobs in the medical world. Some work directly with families by doing checkups, giving shots, and prescribing medications. Others choose to become surgeons, who go inside the human body to treat sicknesses and fix what's broken. Whatever they decide to do, doctors are the leaders of the medical team, and their job is to keep you healthy. Debi Thomas is one such doctor.

At just five years of age, Debi had two dreams—to be a doctor, and to be a figure skater. She was too young for medicine, so she started figure skating. Her mom used to drive her more than 100

DID YOU KNOW...

Physicians can get certified in over 130 different medical specialties.

miles a day from school to the ice rink and back home. Debi showed lots of talent on the rink. By the time she was nine, she was already taking lessons and winning competitions. At age 10, she signed on with coach Alex McGowan. Together, they began to train for the Olympics.

As a young African-American figure skater, Debi was often discriminated against by her judges. They would give her competitors better scores just because of her skin color. Debi did not let this affect her though. She kept going, and won the silver medal at the national novice finals when she was just 12 years old. A few years later, Debi won the national and world championships in the same year, while she was

SKATING TO SUCCESS

Debi smashed barriers for women and African Americans in the rink.

a full-time student. This was an amazing feat because it takes an incredible amount of time to train for this level of competition. It is very difficult to manage being a competitive athlete and a good student, but Debi was determined to do both. Although she loved competing, she never lost sight of her goal to become a doctor.

Just two years later, Debi became the first African American to win a medal at the Winter Olympics in 1988 in Calgary, Canada. She took the bronze in women's figure skating. However, despite her success, she decided to end her figure skating career after the Olympics so she could focus on her medical studies. And she did.

Debi graduated with a degree in engineering from Stanford University, one of the top universities in the U.S. She then went on to study medicine at another top school, Northwestern University. Today, she is a practicing orthopedic surgeon. She specializes in knee and hip

DID YOU KNOW...

Debi comes from a very educated family—both of her parents are computer professionals and her brother is an astrophysicist.

Debi had to balance studying and training in order to reach her goal of becoming a doctor.

replacements. Because she is a doctor, Debi is committed to helping others. In fact, she even does that when she's not working.

Debi recently took a trip to Nepal to give free knee replacements to women who don't have the right medical care. The knee is the biggest joint in the body, and when it gets damaged it can cause people a lot of pain. Often, these people can no longer participate in the activities they love, like sports. Sometimes, they can't even walk. A knee replacement allows them to get back on their feet pain-free. Debi understands just how meaningful an active lifestyle can be. Her trip to Nepal allowed her to give the opportunities she had as an athlete back to those who are less fortunate.

On top of having a successful medical career, Debi was inducted into the figure skating hall of fame in 2000,

ON THE ROAD AGAIN

Millions of people suffer from knee problems every year. Debi does procedures like knee replacements, shown below, to help them get back on their feet.

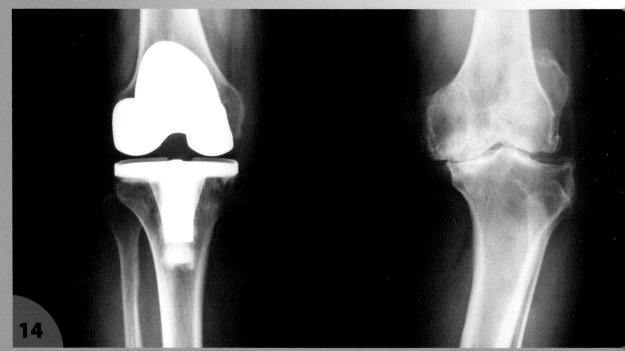

proving that women have the brains and the brawn to be world-class athletes as well as doctors. Debi worked her way

up to become a successful orthopedic surgeon. Others, like Regina Benjamin, are also reaching the highest level of medicine.

Regina's career in medicine began when she was in college. Before then, she had no interest in medicine. "I had never seen a black doctor before," said Regina, "…so I did not have an idea that I wanted to be one… I had never really thought about it at all." Once she did think of it, however, nothing got in her way.

Regina graduated from medical school and focused her efforts on family care. She founded a small rural health clinic in Bayou La Batre, Alabama, where most of her patients were below the poverty line. As a result, many of them couldn't pay for their medical treatment. Regina had to work for years in emergency rooms and nursing homes to keep her clinic open so that she could help people in need. But shortage of money wasn't

the only problem she faced. In 1998, disaster struck: Hurricane Georges destroyed the clinic. Instead of giving up, Regina made house calls for her patients, using her car until her clinic was rebuilt. In 2005, disaster struck again. Hurricane Katrina devastated Bayou La Batre, destroying her clinic a second time. Once again, Regina rolled up her sleeves and continued to serve her patients. Her hard work and determination to treat her patients, despite all these obstacles, are what led President Barack Obama to make Regina surgeon general.

Regina Benjamin served as the 18th Surgeon General of the United States. The surgeon general advises the president about scientific and public health issues. They also command the Commissioned Corps, a group of 6,500 health professionals who are on call 24 hours a day.

Hurricane Katrina caused billions of dollars of damage and left many people homeless in places like Bayou La Batre and New Orleans.

In an emergency, they can be dispatched to anywhere in the country at a moment's notice. On top of all this, the surgeon general is responsible for educating the American public about health issues, and promoting healthy lifestyles. The surgeon general must be chosen by the president and approved by the Senate. Regina was appointed by President Obama. Before her, there were only three women who had served as surgeon general.

AN APPLE A DAY KEEPS THE DOCTOR AWAY

As surgeon general, Regina focused on preventive care —particularly on raising healthier children.

As surgeon general, Regina focused her efforts on preventive care. Her mother, father, and brother all died of what she calls "preventable diseases." She believes that nobody should have to die from a disease that can be prevented. Regina also believes that people should enjoy becoming and staying fit. She published papers about how Americans can eat healthy, exercise more, and manage stress. She also released reports about the dangers of smoking to-bacco.

Her work as surgeon general helped to shift the country's focus from simple treatment to actual disease-prevention.

Through all of her accomplishments, Regina was always driven to make a difference. "I hope to make a difference one person at a time," she said. "By making a patient feel better, [or] by telling a mother that her baby is going to be okay." Regina proved that women have the compassion, dedication, and perseverance to reach the highest levels of medicine.

Female physicians are finally establishing their place in the medical community. They aren't the only ones making a difference in the medical world, however. Nurses, like Clara Barton, have also played a role in opening up the medical world to women.

CHAPTER 3
NURSES

Nurses are the largest group of medical workers in the United States. Unlike many other health professions, nursing is female-dominated. More than 90% of registered nurses in the US are women. These women work hard every day to care for their patients, families, and communities. Women were not always allowed these opportunities, however. They were expected to get married and stay home. Women like Clara Barton fought hard to break this trend and to bring women into the workforce.

Clara Barton was always looking for ways to help people. When she was just 11 years old, her brother was badly injured when he fell in the family's barn. Over the next three years, she

DID YOU KNOW...
In the United States, there are four nurses for every doctor.

took care of him and learned how to administer all of his medical treatment. Even when doctors gave up trying to fix him, Clara continued to care for her brother. Thanks to her determination, he made a full recovery. This was the kind of compassionate, persevering attitude that she would take into her adult life.

Having grown up around her brother and male cousins, Clara was never intimidated by men. She believed

NUMBER-ONE NURSE

Nurses are some of the hardest working medical professionals. Without them, doctors could not keep up with everybody who needs to be treated.

Just like Elizabeth Blackwell, Clara was featured on a U.S. postage stamp in 1948.

that women could do everything that men could. She would go horseback riding with her male cousins, who were surprised at how well she kept up. In fact, her mother was concerned that she needed to get in touch with her feminine side. Clara never let other people's ideas of femininity get in her way, however. She used her own independent personality to pave the way for women everywhere she went.

Clara began her career as a schoolteacher. She was a gifted teacher, and was especially good at controlling the rowdy boys in her class. She even opened her own school in Bordentown, New Jersey in 1852. The attendance at her school grew very quickly, and in less than a year Clara was teaching more than 600 students. She was so successful that the residents of Bordentown voted to build her a better school in 1853. When the new school opened, however, the board

hired a man as principal instead of Clara. They even decided to pay him twice as much as she had been paid. Clara became frustrated, but didn't let this decision get in her way. She left teaching to pursue a job in the U.S. government.

When Clara made her decision to work in the government, no woman had ever worked there before. She hoped that by getting a job she would create new opportunities for women everywhere. Against all odds, Clara got a job as a clerk, with the same pay as her male coworkers. Unfortunately, many Americans at the time were against women working in government. Their protests eventually got Clara fired from her job. Even though the American people were against her, Clara did not let their opinions get in her way. She returned to her job in the government with lower pay, determined to pave the way for other women. When the Civil War broke out a few months later, however, Clara found her true calling in medicine.

The first soldiers arrived in Washington, D.C. a few months after Clara returned to her job in the government. It quickly became apparent that there was too little medical staff and too many soldiers. Some of them were already badly wounded and needed medical attention. She started taking supplies to the men of the 6th Massachusetts Infantry unit. After meeting some of the soldiers, she was horrified to realize many of them were once her students. This drove her to brave the front lines to help soldiers on the battlefield. She petitioned the government until they let her become a battlefield nurse. On the front lines, she earned the title "Angel of the Battlefield" because of her courage. One time, she was even grazed by a bullet while she was treating a soldier.

After the Civil War, Clara took a trip to Europe.

FIGHT FOR FREEDOM

The Civil War was the biggest conflict in American history. Many soldiers on both sides were killed and many more wounded.

While she was there, she was introduced to the Red Cross in Switzerland. The Red Cross is an organization that provides help to victims of war and natural disasters. She was inspired by the work that they were doing in Europe, and came back home to found the American Red Cross. It was officially approved in 1881 by the President of the United States. Since then, the American Red Cross has helped millions of victims of war, hurricanes, tornadoes, and other disasters. Today, the Red Cross can be found all over the U.S., with offices in every state. Clara wasn't the only woman who found her passion for medicine in the military, however. Hazel Johnson-Brown, the first female African-American army general, also devoted her life to helping others through nursing.

Hazel Johnson-Brown was born in October 1927, in Pennsylvania. She grew up in a large family, with four brothers and two sisters. Her parents taught her the value of hard work at a very young age. At just 12 years old, Hazel had a job and did things like cook, clean, wash, and iron at home. At the same time, she set a goal to become a nurse. When she first applied to nursing school, however, she was rejected because of racial prejudice. But the family nurse, a white woman, saw Hazel's true potential. She helped Hazel move to New York, where she was accepted into Harlem Hospital School of Nursing.

It didn't take long for Hazel's fellow students to see her natural leadership ability. After she graduated in 1950, they suggested that she join the Army. She met with a recruiter, and signed up for what she thought would just be two years. Instead, it was the start of a career that lasted almost 30 years.

Hazel rose through the ranks of the Army very quickly. Not only was she a natural leader, but she also was always seeking more education. Over the course of her career in the Army, Hazel got four degrees from top colleges, such as Columbia University and the Catholic University of America. She also worked overseas in places like Japan and Korea, always impressing her bosses with her eagerness to learn. It came as no surprise when she was appointed as chief of the

PROUD TO SERVE

The military is a great opportunity for female nurses to serve their country.

Army Nurse Corps and promoted to brigadier general. She was the first African-American woman to achieve either position. "Race is an incidence of birth," she said when she was promoted. "I hope the criterion for selection didn't include race, but competence."

RISING THROUGH THE RANKS

Hazel believed that neither race nor gender should be a factor when hiring someone for a job. All that matters are their qualifications and willingness to work.

As chief, Hazel had many accomplishments. Many of them focused on helping Army nurses get educations and educate others, a value her parents taught her. She created scholarships to help Army nursing students pay for nursing school. She started nursing summer camps for Army cadets in college. She promoted

Army nurses getting higher education in real universities instead of military programs.

She even held conferences that encouraged Army nurses to do research and publish their findings. Hazel gave opportunities to Army nurses that they never had before. Her hard work and dedication opened many doors for women in nursing today.

While doctors and nurses get a lot of the attention, many other medical workers work hard to help people as well. These include physical therapists, paramedics, and athletic trainers, just to name a few. Just like being a doctor, however, these professions were not always open to women. Even today, many of the women working in these fields don't get paid as much as men. It has taken the work of people like Lee Clout to help reverse these trends.

CHAPTER 4
PARAMEDICS AND PHYSICAL THERAPISTS

One of the most important parts of the medical world is Emergency Medical Services, or EMS. EMS is responsible for responding to medical emergencies and moving patients to hospitals. If you've ever seen an ambulance driving down the road with sirens blaring, that's an EMS team doing its job. Many of the people who work in ambulances are called paramedics. The job of a paramedic is very demanding. They must be able to carry people to and from ambulances. Because of this, many people thought women couldn't handle the job. Lee Clout proved them wrong.

Lee was the first female paramedic for the New South Wales Ambulance

DID YOU KNOW...

Before the modern ambulance, EMS used to use hearses—the same vehicles used by funeral homes—to transport patients.

Service in Australia. However, when she joined in 1979, she had no idea she was opening a whole new door for women. "I wasn't aware there had been no females in the service previously," she said. She wasn't afraid of the work paramedics did, though. She was already trained as a nurse and had volunteered during World War II.

FIRST RESPONDERS

Paramedics work on the front lines of medicine. They are the first people to arrive on the scene of an emergency.

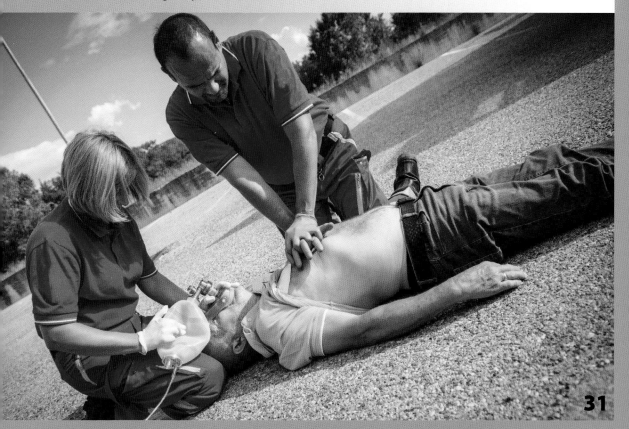

EMS often works side by side with firefighters during emergencies.

She wanted to continue helping people in the medical industry. At 5'9", she was even taller than many of her male coworkers. She easily passed the height and the strength tests, but wasn't so easily accepted by her coworkers.

New South Wales Ambulance Service was not prepared for Lee Clout's arrival. They gave her the same uniform the men used, which was much too big. They also gave her heels and a handbag, which she got rid of quickly. "The first time [I wore the heels], I fell into the back of a wagon because my heel was caught. After that I got a pair of boots, the same as the men." Some of those men were equally unprepared for her arrival. "There were men who didn't want females in the service, but that made me even more determined to say, 'We can do the job—I can do the job.'" Lee didn't care what the guys thought—she was there to do her job and do it well. And she did.

Lee didn't only want to prove that she could be a paramedic. She wanted to prove that all women could. Her work showed that not only could women be paramedics, but also that the service desperately needed them. Female paramedics related much better to female patients. One of her male colleagues said, "The biggest thing I noticed was the fact that she was welcomed so openly by the patients, especially female patients. That's when I realized how big a void in the service there had actually been."

Just like her heels, Lee

Without people like Lee Clout, many patients would never make it to the hospital.

threw out the stereotypes men had about women in EMS. Her work inspired many women to pursue their dreams of becoming paramedics and helping people. However, not all jobs in the medical field deal with emergencies. Many women, like physical therapist Judy Seto, are finding success in other branches of medicine.

DID YOU KNOW...

Paramedics have to be ready for any situation. Many undergo more than 10,000 hours of training.

Physical therapists can be described as the masters of human movement. Their job is to restore mobility in people who have been injured. They work in a variety of settings, but lately many are being employed by sports teams. Judy Seto is one such physical therapist.

Judy didn't always want to be a physical therapist. She first discovered the profession when she was in college. Her friend's dad had a stroke, and she went to go visit him in the hospital. It was there that she met his physical therapist. He told her about the opportunities physical therapists had to work with all different types of people. She was fascinated by sports medicine, and wanted to work with athletes. She was a pre-medical student at the time, but quickly switched her interest to physical therapy.

In order to become the successful physical therapist she is today, Judy had to get a lot of education. She received two degrees from the University of California, Los Angeles in her undergraduate years. She went on to get her master's and doctorate in physical therapy,

Kobe Bryant attributes much of his athletic success to Judy Seto's care.

and even further to get many specialization certificates. These certificates, like certified strength and conditioning specialist, help Judy to work more closely with athletes. Her determination to always improve herself definitely paid off. The Los Angeles Lakers saw Judy's potential and began working with her right away.

Judy has been an incredible asset during her 20 years working with the Lakers. She has a very unique method of dealing with athletes. Instead of looking at one body part at a time, Judy focuses her efforts on the athletes' full body alignment. She takes the whole athlete into consideration. She makes sure that everything is working together so that nothing breaks down on game day. Her unique approach has prevented numerous injuries amongst the players. When asked about how much of an impact Judy had on the team, Lakers player Kobe Bryant said, "Enormous. It's really huge." In fact, Judy has developed a strong relationship with the Lakers' star guard. She has helped him become one of the best players in the league.

One of the key reasons for Kobe's extremely success-ful career is his lack of major injuries. He first worked with Judy when he hurt his ankle in the early 2000s. She helped him recover and get back on the court. Kobe was impressed with her ability to understand

DID YOU KNOW...

Judy has two bachelors degrees, two master's degrees, and a doctorate of physical therapy. She is also a certified sports medicine, orthopedic, and strength and conditioning specialist.

Physical therapists treat a wide range of problems. Vertigo, or moments of dizziness, is caused by an ear dysfunction, of all things, and can be treated by physical therapy.

and solve all the problems he was having. He worked hard to get Judy a full-time spot on staff. In 2011, she became the first woman to work full-time with an NBA team. That year, the Lakers had an injury-free season. She has since become a treasured member of the Lakers.

CRITICAL CARE

Judy (middle right) is an essential member of the Lakers team. She's even included in their team photos.

CHAPTER 5
CONCLUSION

Women have proven they have what it takes to make it in the medical field. They are doctors, nurses, physical therapists, paramedics, and more. Where they were once forbidden to work, they have become essential members of the medical team. Now, it's hard to imagine a world without women in medicine.

Thanks to the work of women like Elizabeth Blackwell, Regina Benjamin, and Hazel Johnson-Brown, women were able to reach the highest levels of medicine in America. Debi Thomas proved that women could be professional athletes and doctors. Judy Seto has made the best athletes in the world even better for more than 20 years. Lee Clout destroyed the idea that women weren't strong enough to be paramedics. The work these women have done has

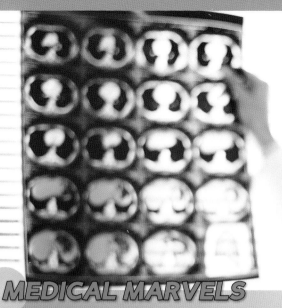

MEDICAL MARVELS

Women are becoming leaders and changing the face of medicine.

set the stage for a more equal future in medicine.

Despite these numerous accomplishments, there is still room for women to grow in the world of medicine. Many women still make less money than men. Some specialties, like surgery, are still dominated by males. It will take the hard work of future pioneers to continue paving the way towards equality. As Elizabeth said, "It is not easy to be a pioneer—but oh, it is fascinating! I would not trade one moment, even the worst moment, for all the riches in the world." The possibilities in medicine are endless, and so are the opportunities for women.